MY COLORING BOOK

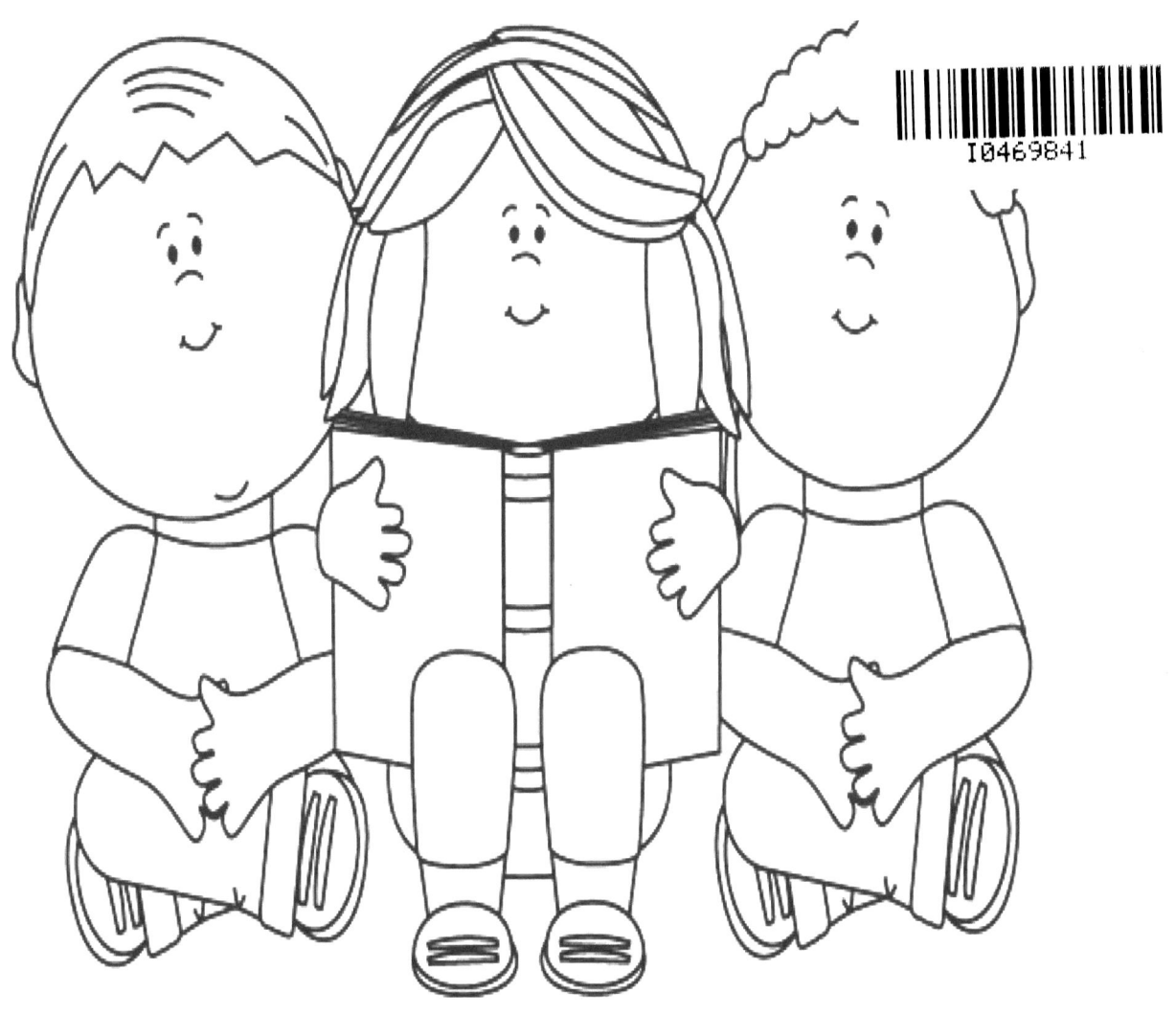

WRITTEN BY: MELISSA L. BRYANT

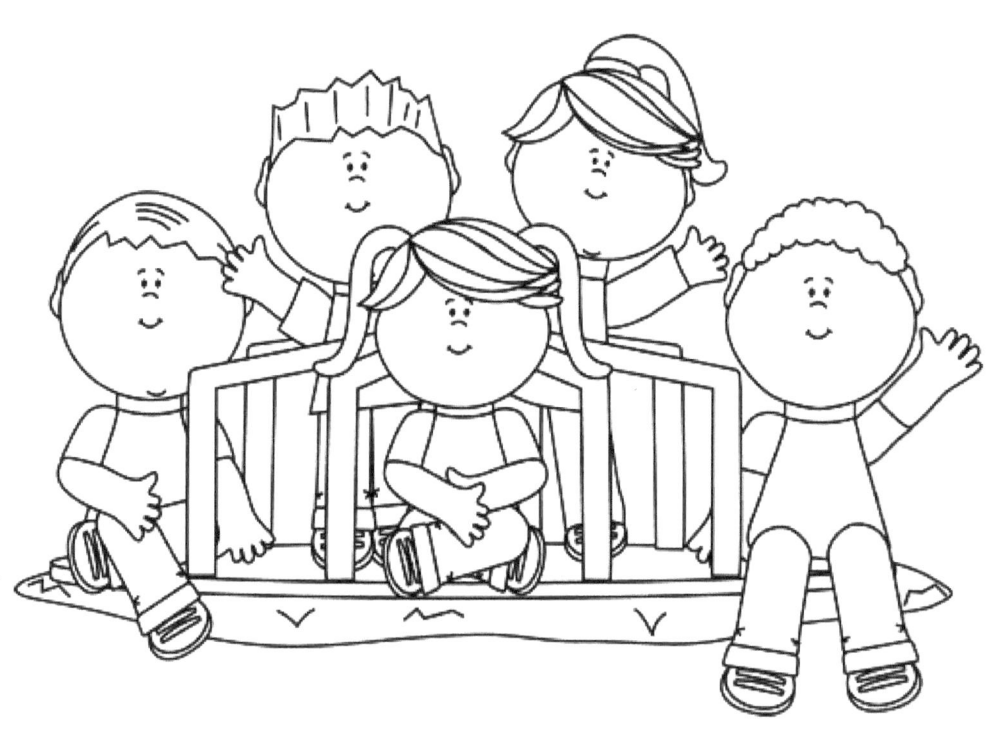

I LOVE HAVING FUN WITH MY FRIENDS.

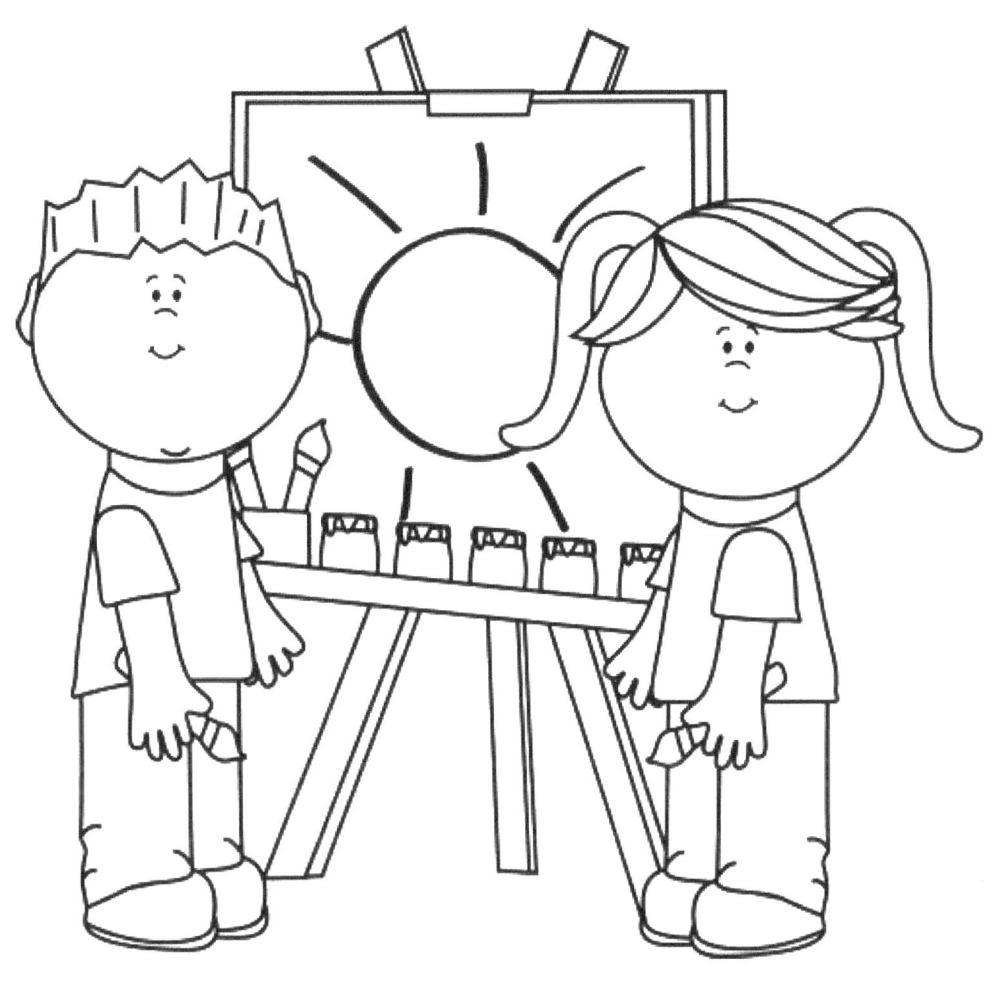

LET'S PAINT THIS PICTURE TIM.

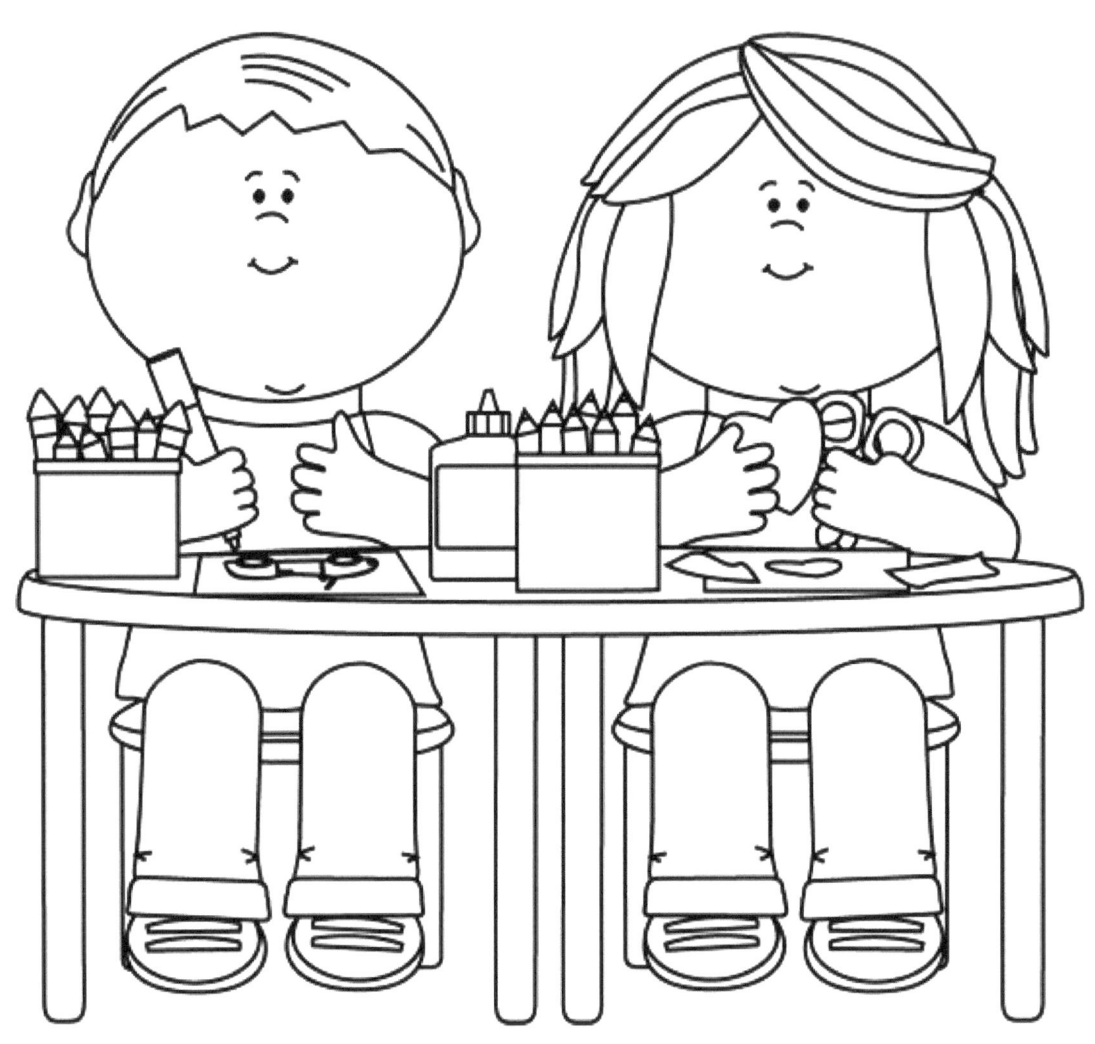

I LOVE ART.

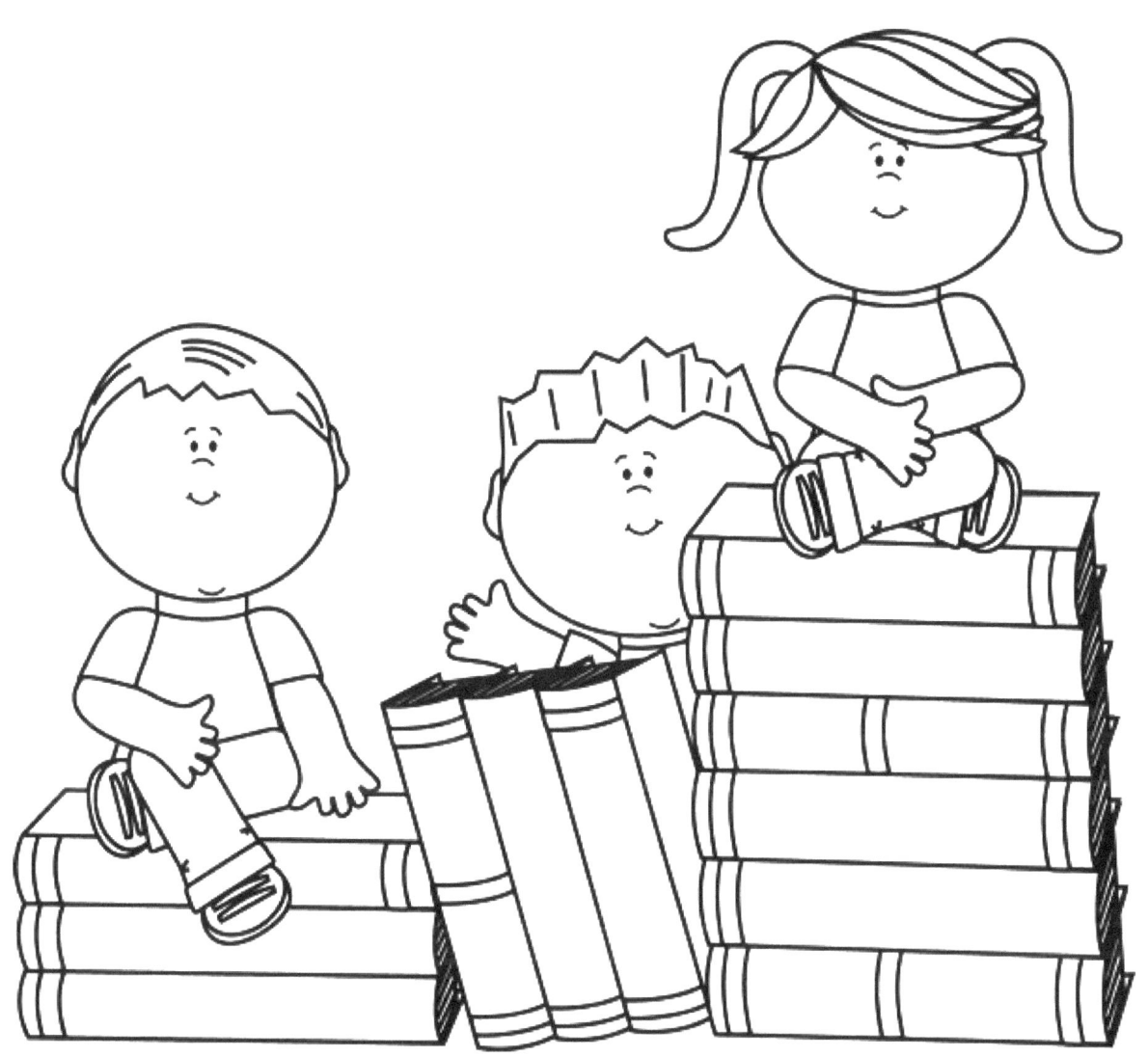

LEARNING IS FUN.

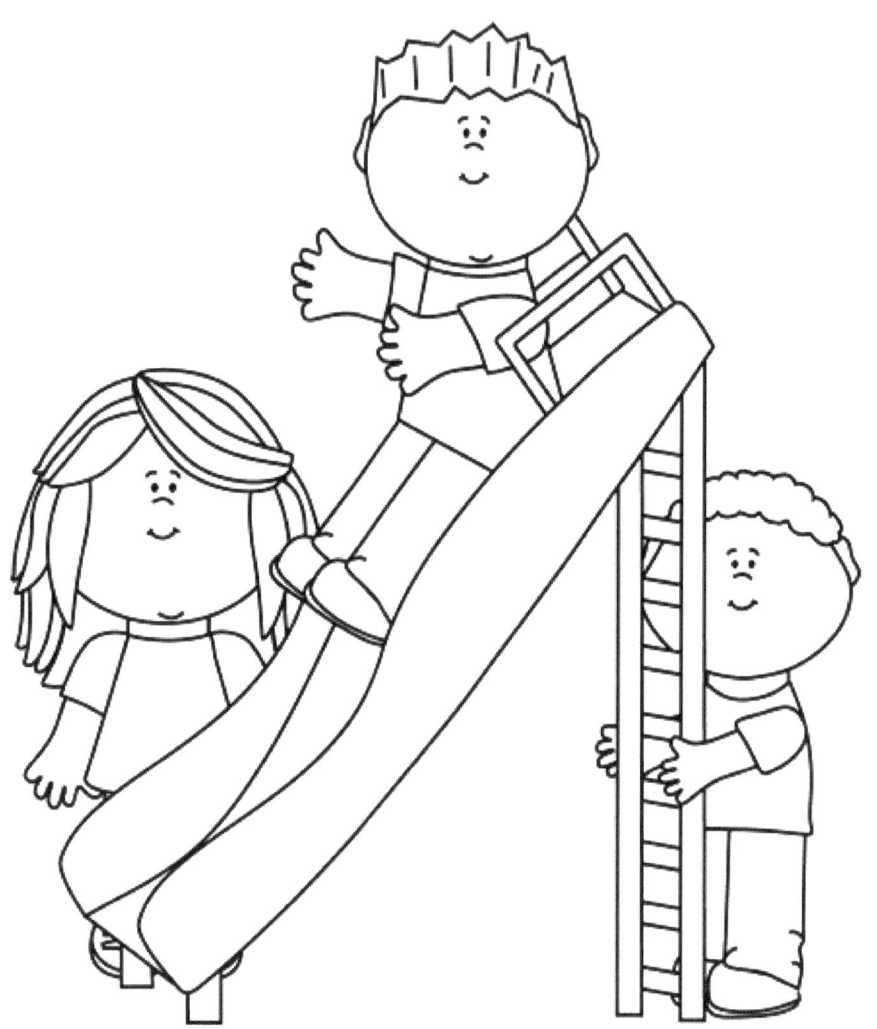

I AM HAVING SO MUCH FUN.

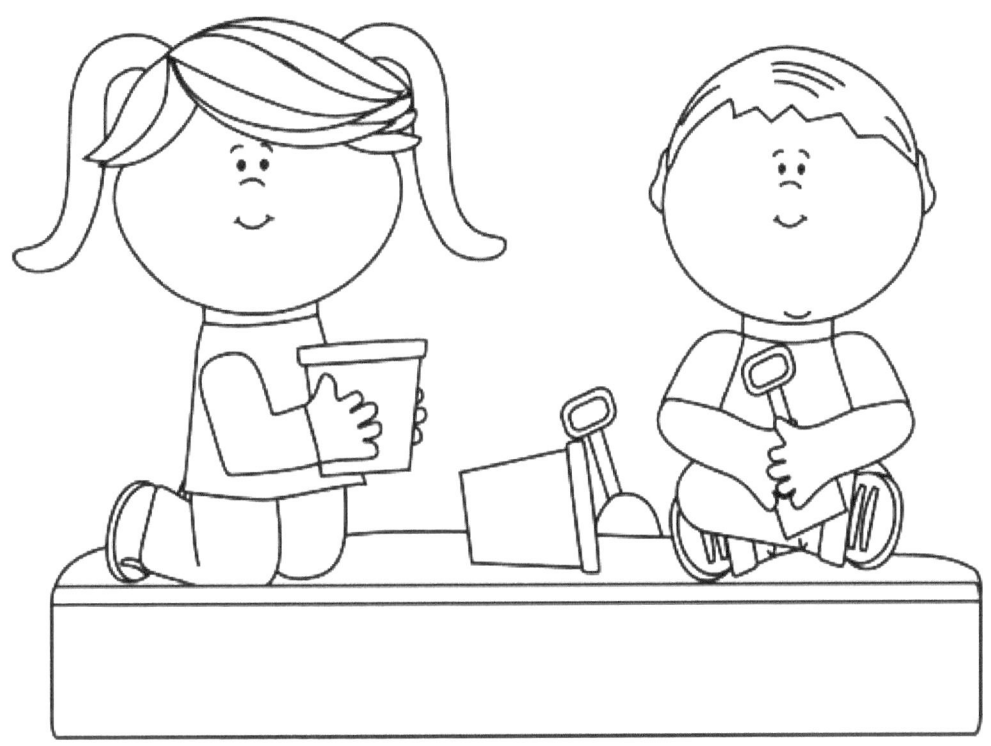

LET'S MAKE SOMETHING WITH THE SAND.

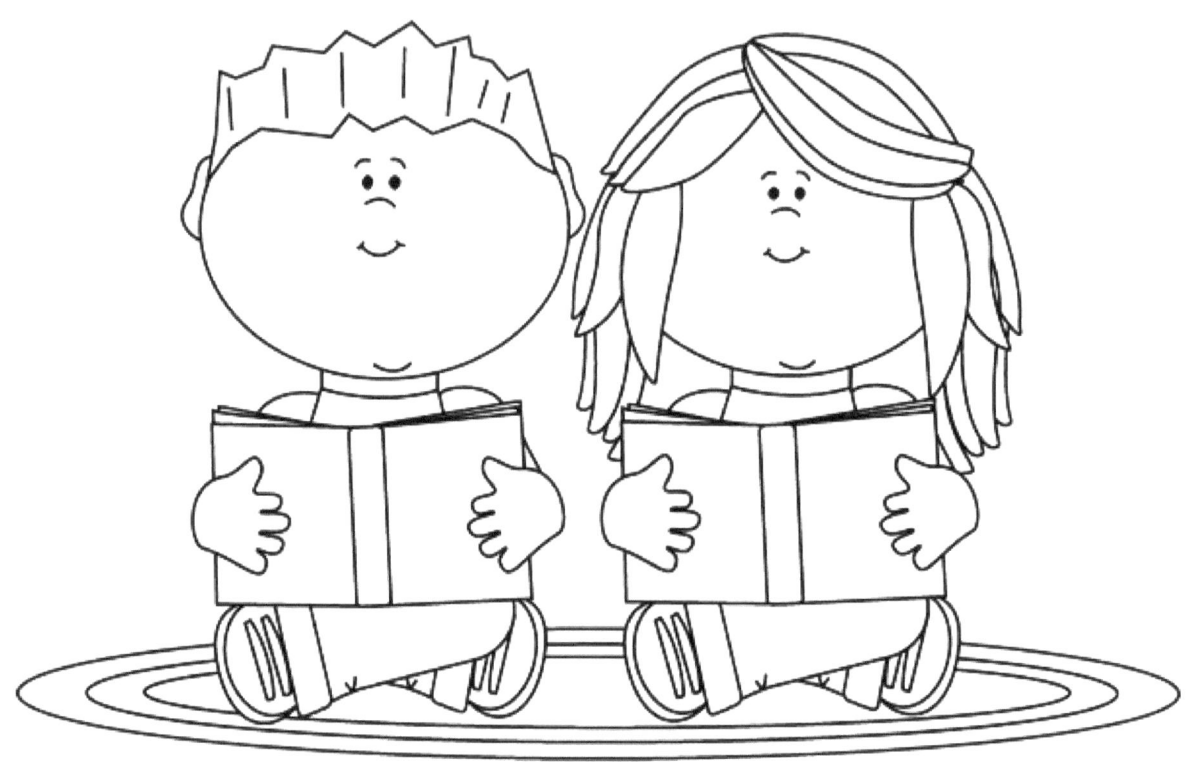

DO YOU LIKE TO READ?

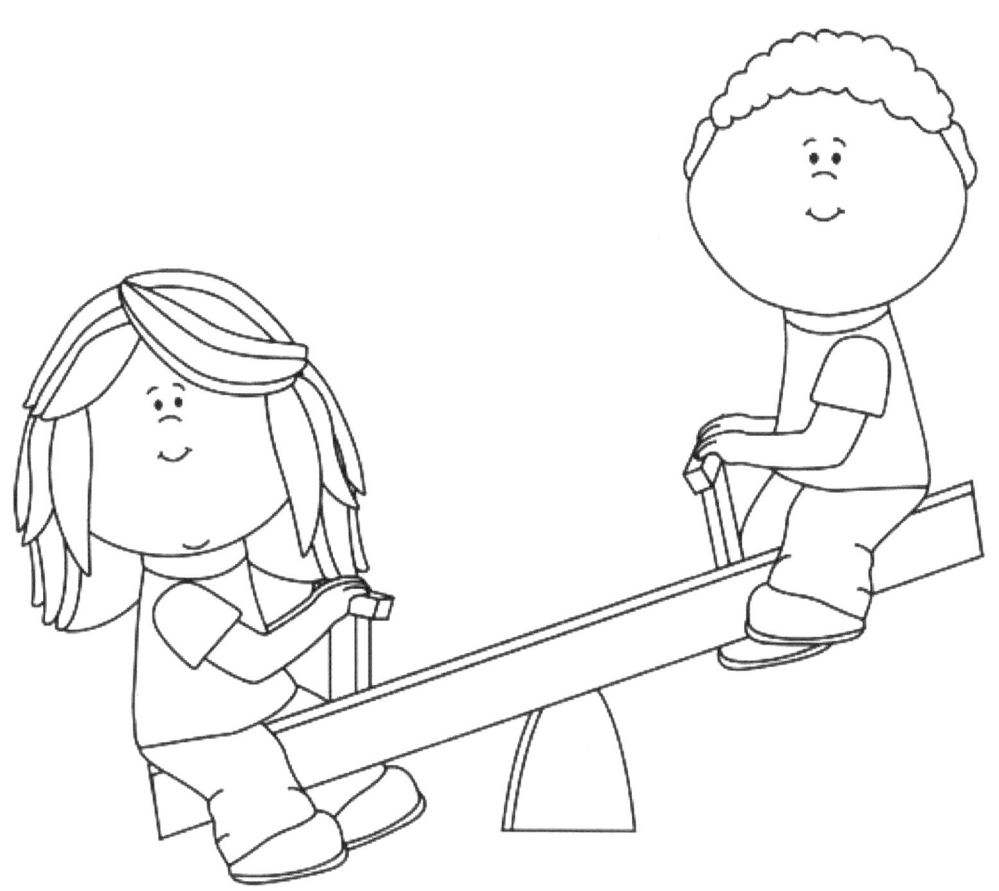

UP AND DOWN! UP AND DOWN WE GO.

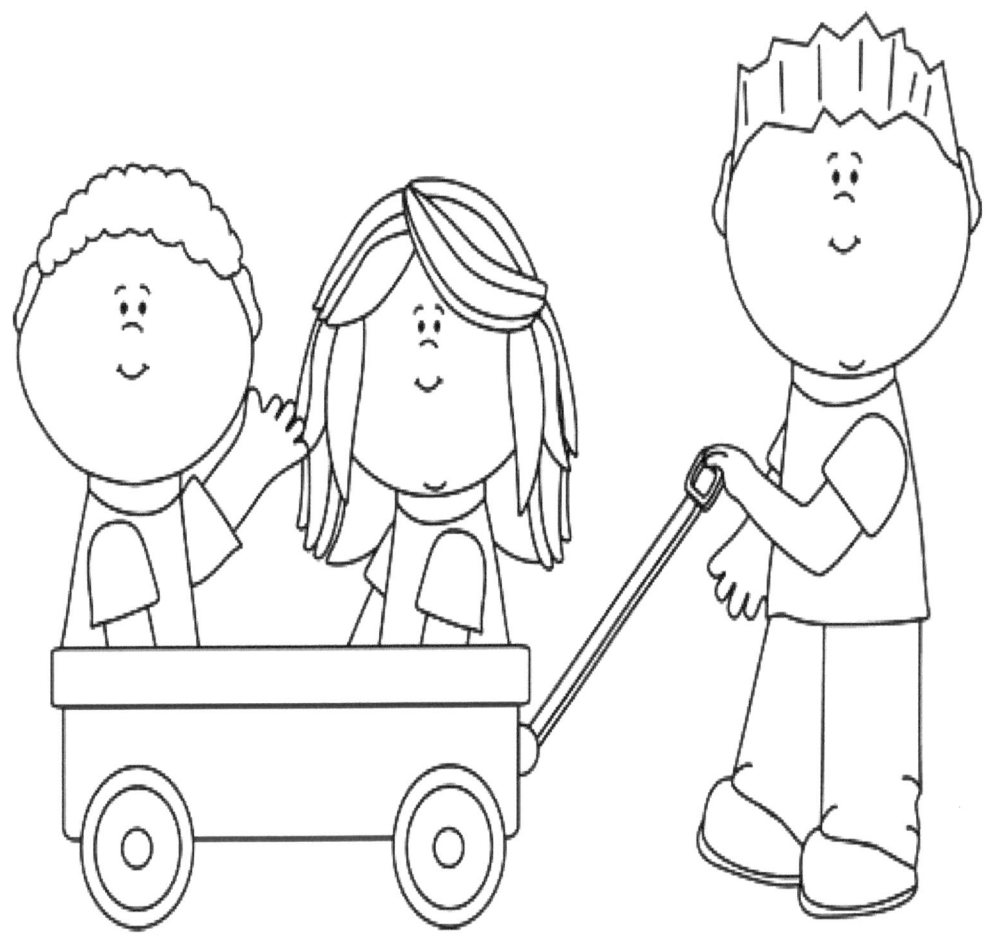

I LOVE PUSHING MY FRIENDS IN THE WAGON.

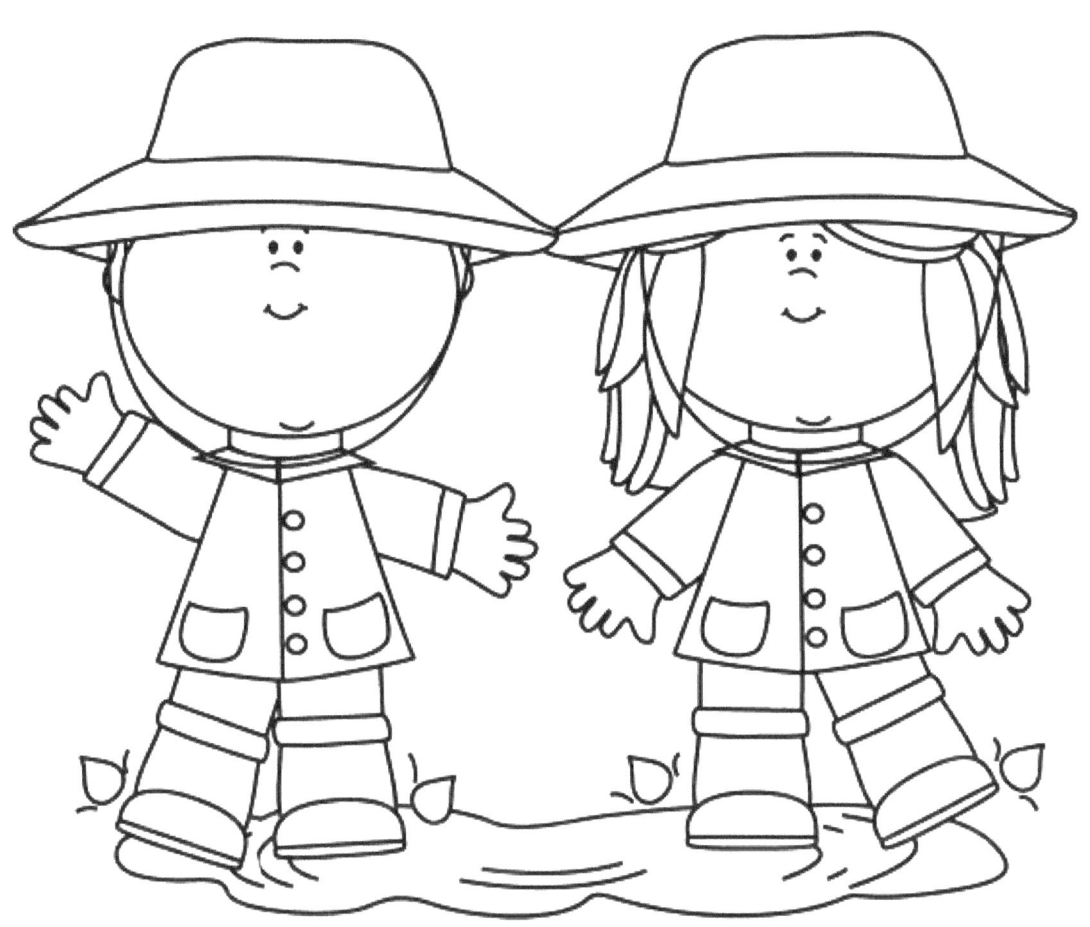

DO YOU LIKE PLAYING IN THE RAIN?

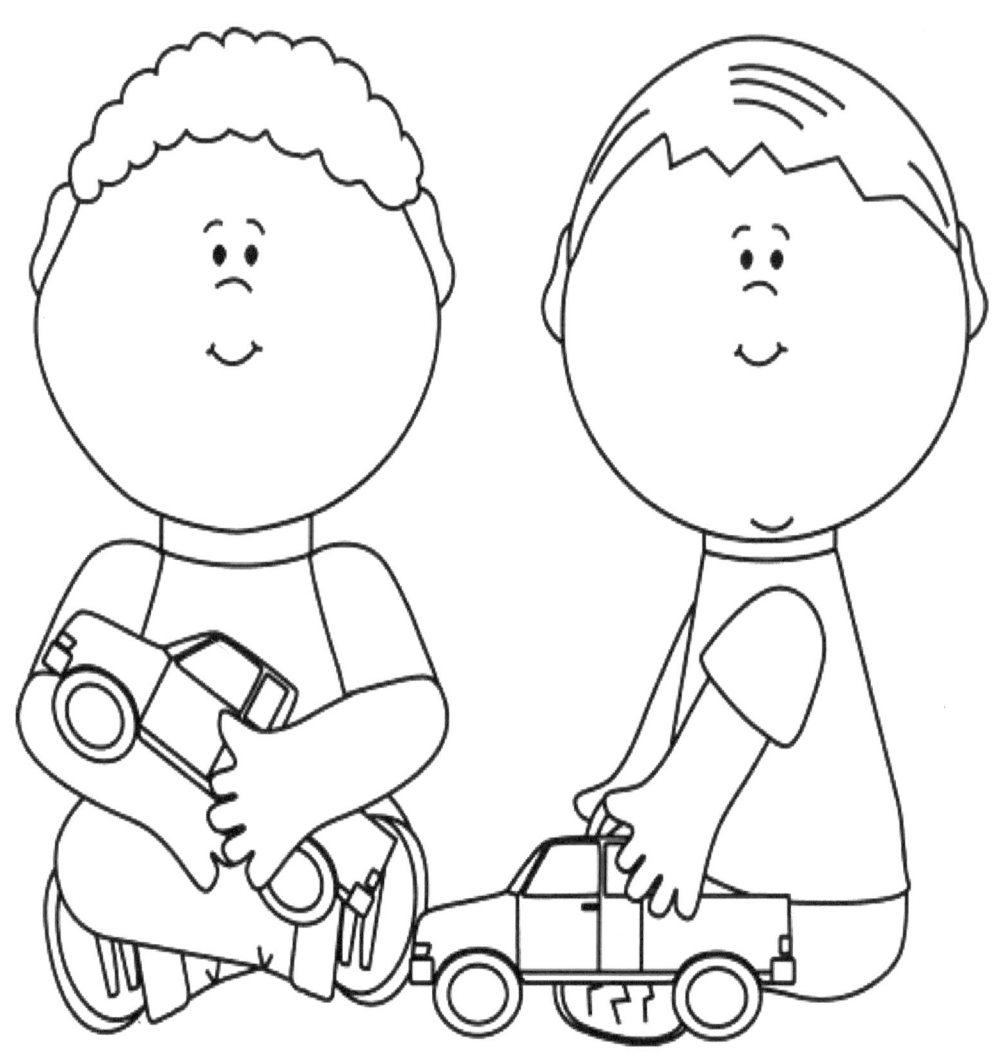

I AM HAVING FUN PLAYING WITH MY FRIEND.

(11)

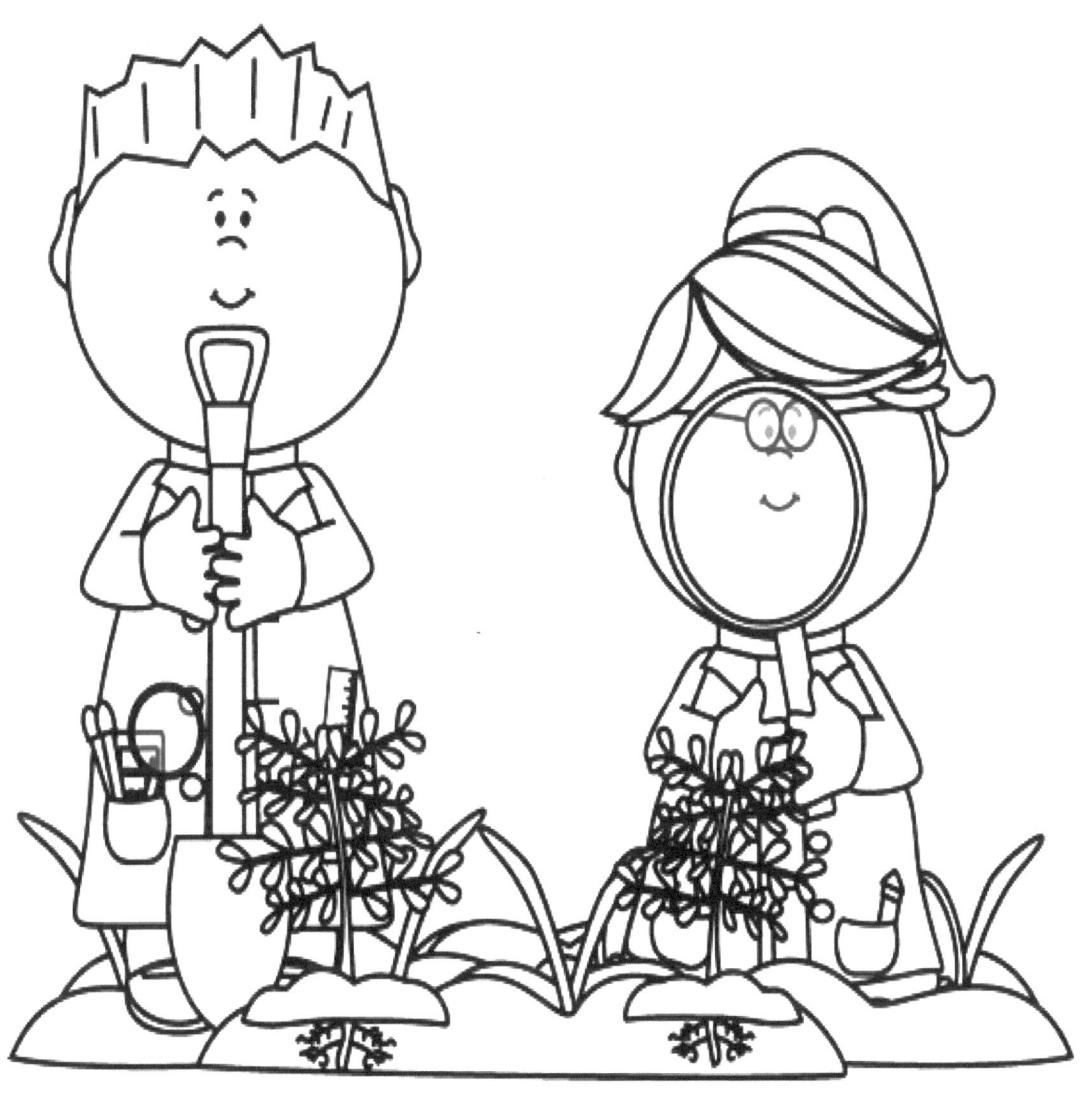

WE ARE TAKING CARE OF THE PLANTS.

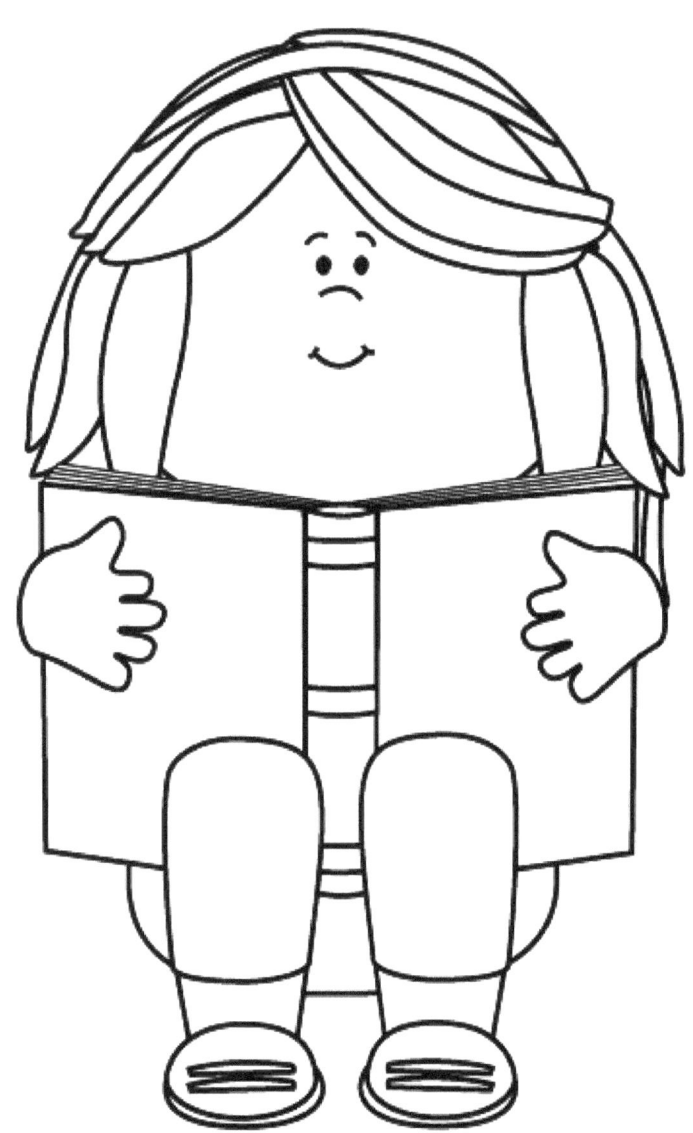

I LOVE TO READ.

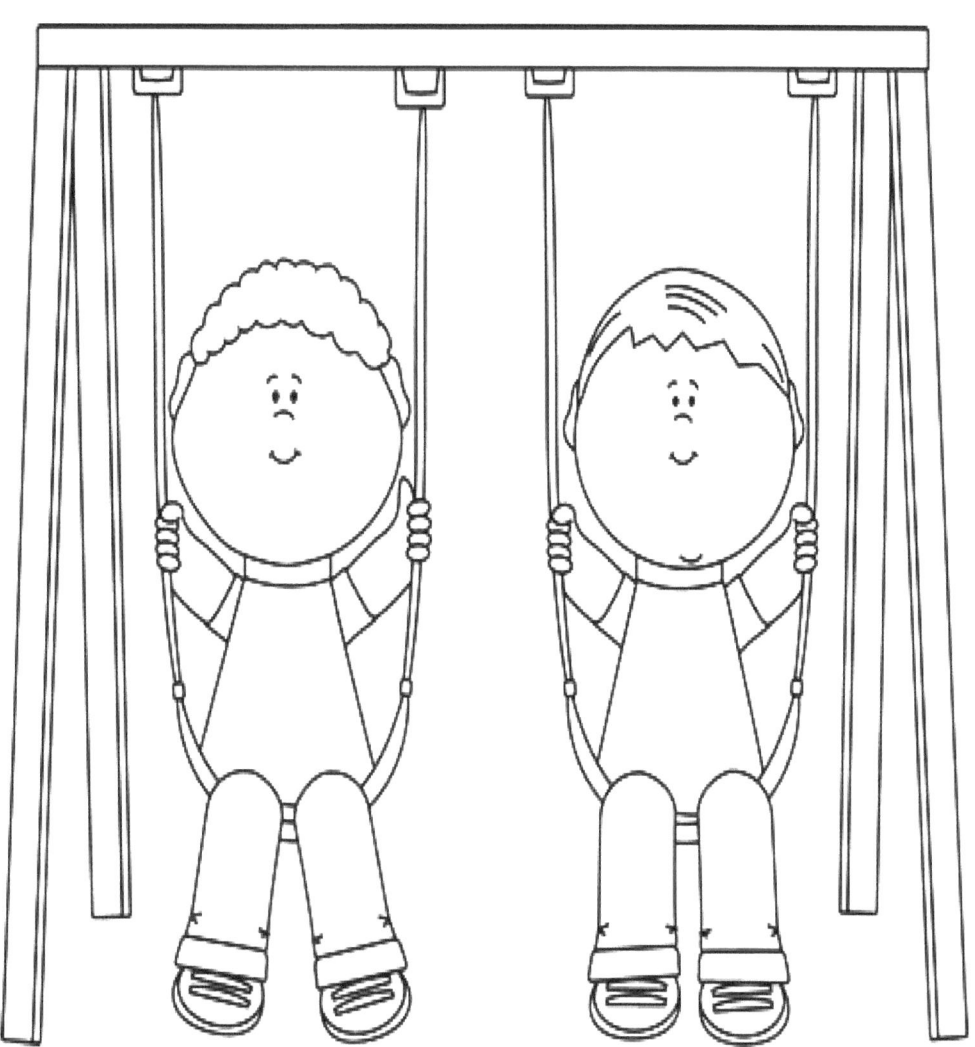

DO YOU LIKE TO SWING?

(14)

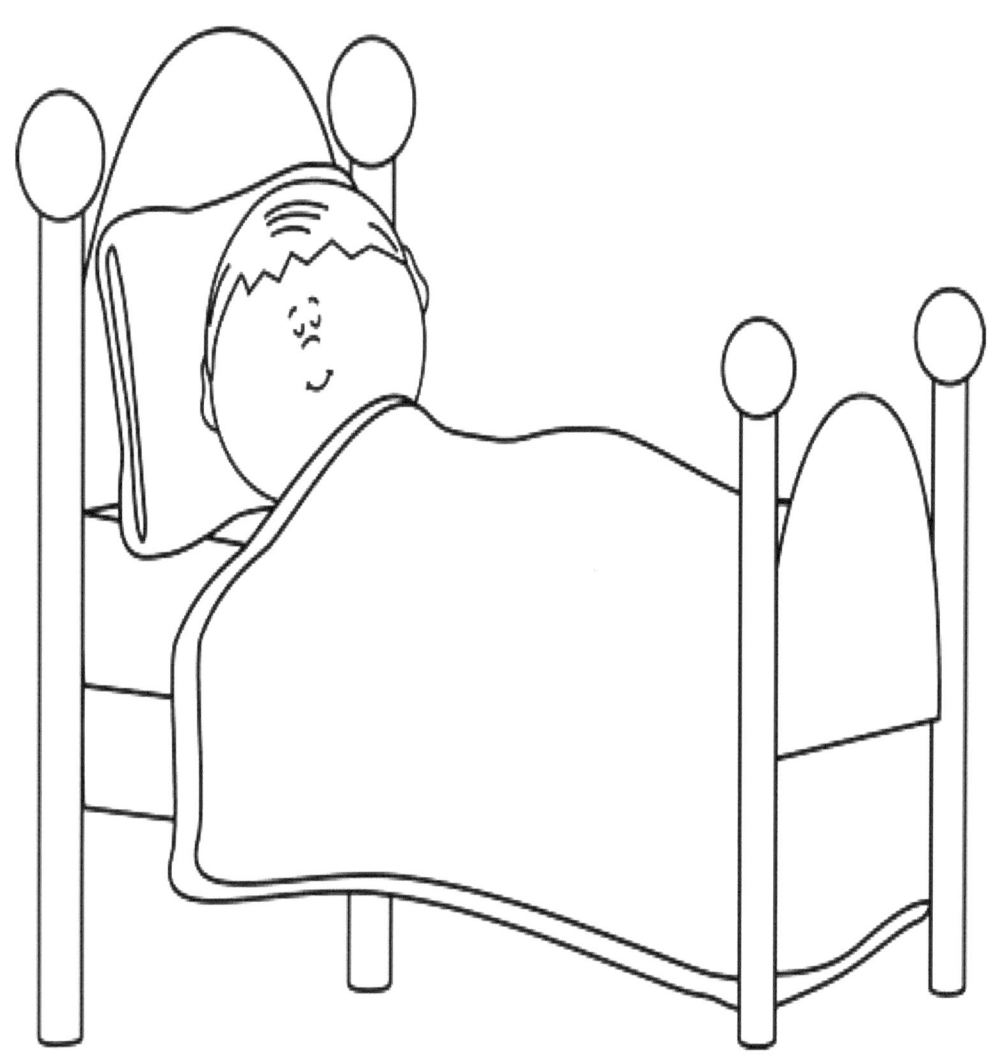

IT'S BED TIME!

(15)

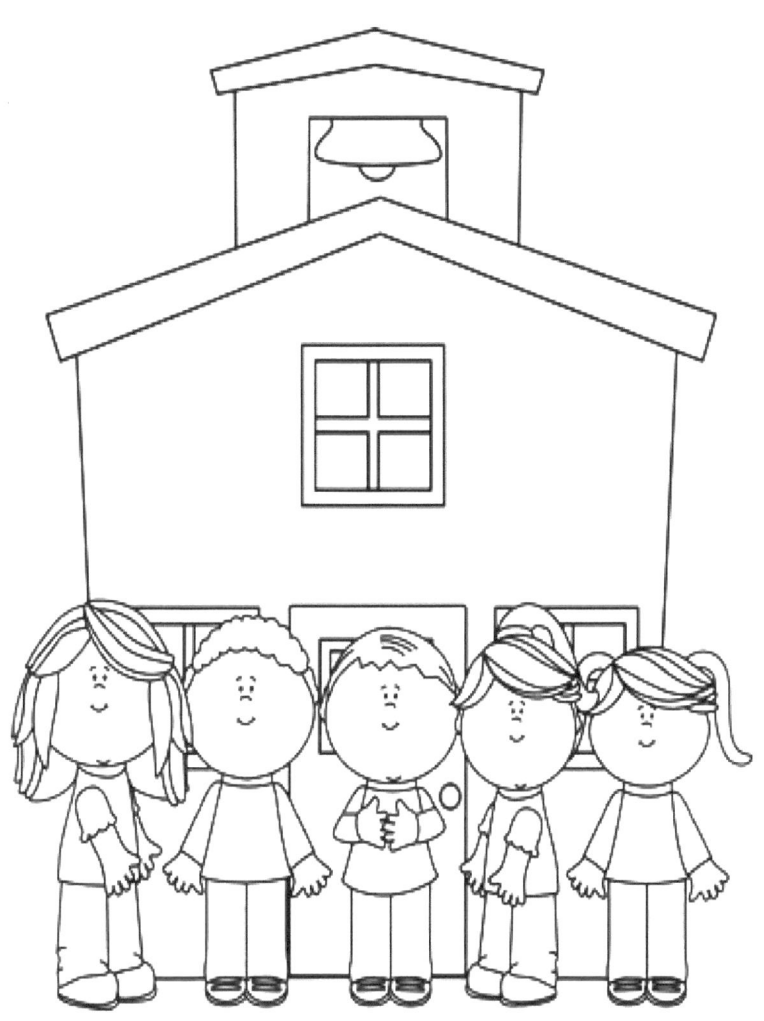

IT'S TIME TO GO TO SCHOOL.

(16)

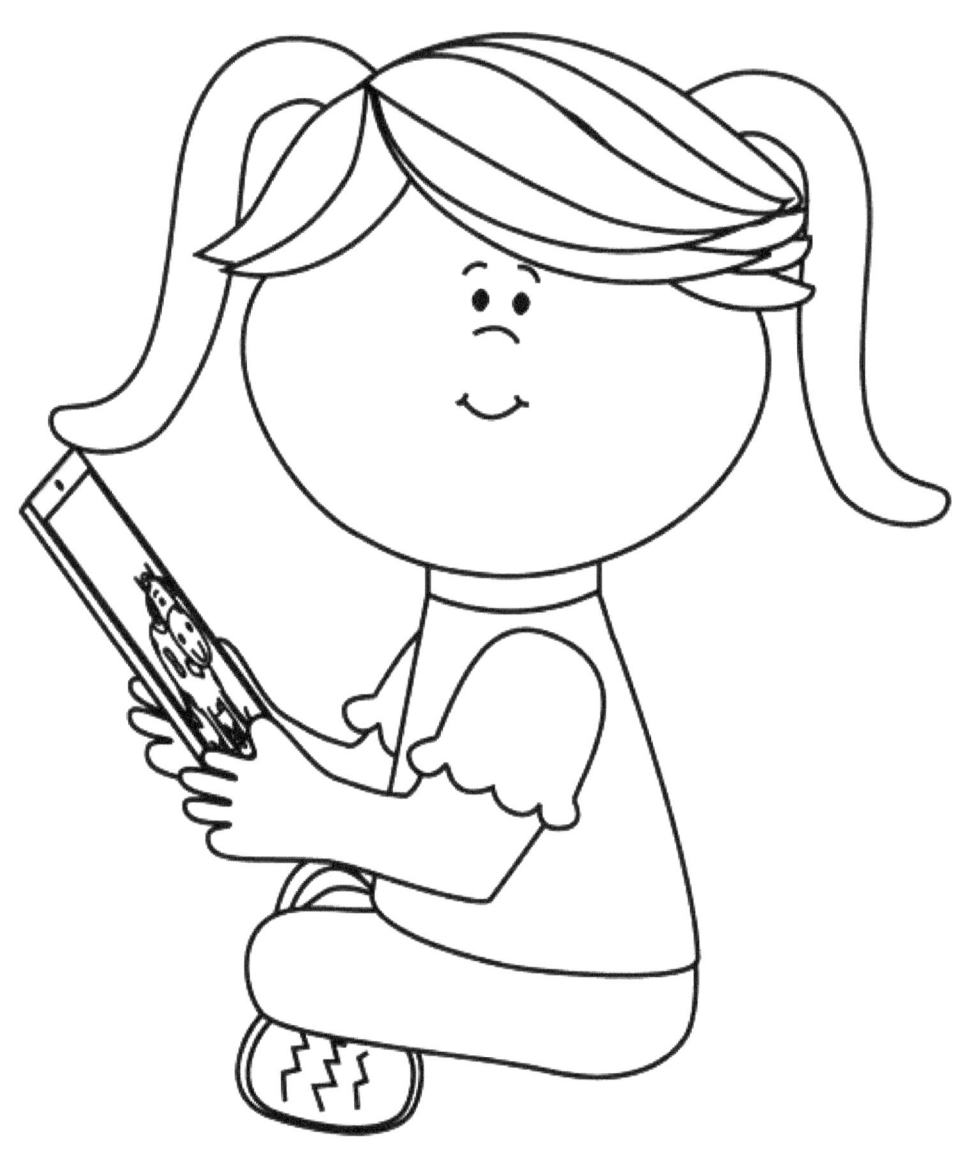

THIS IS A PICTURE OF MY FAMILY.

(17)

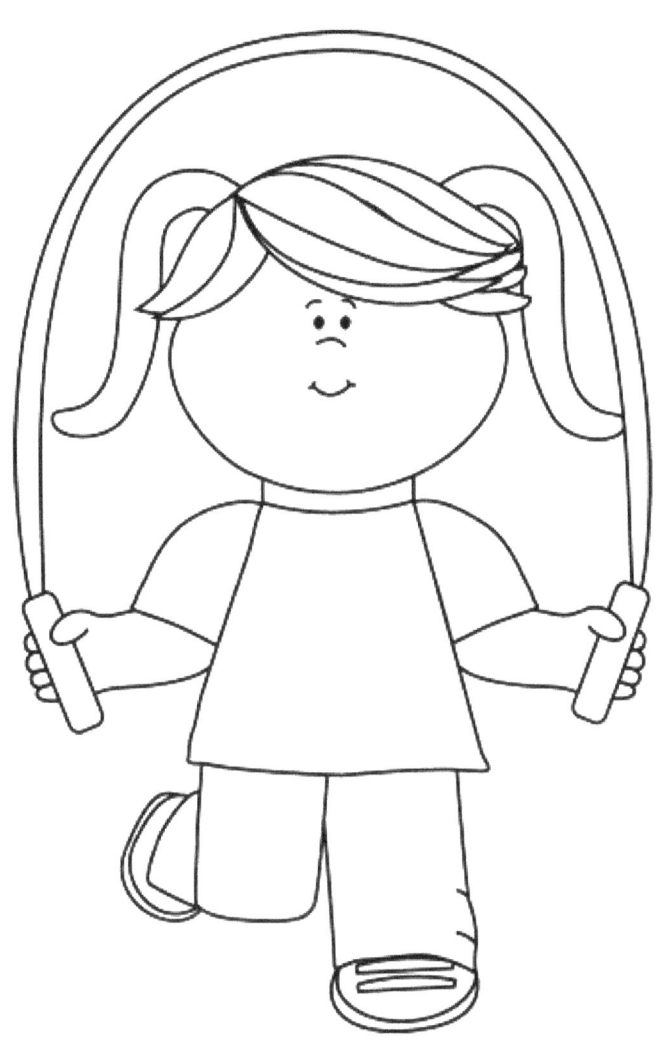

I LIKE TO JUMP ROPE.

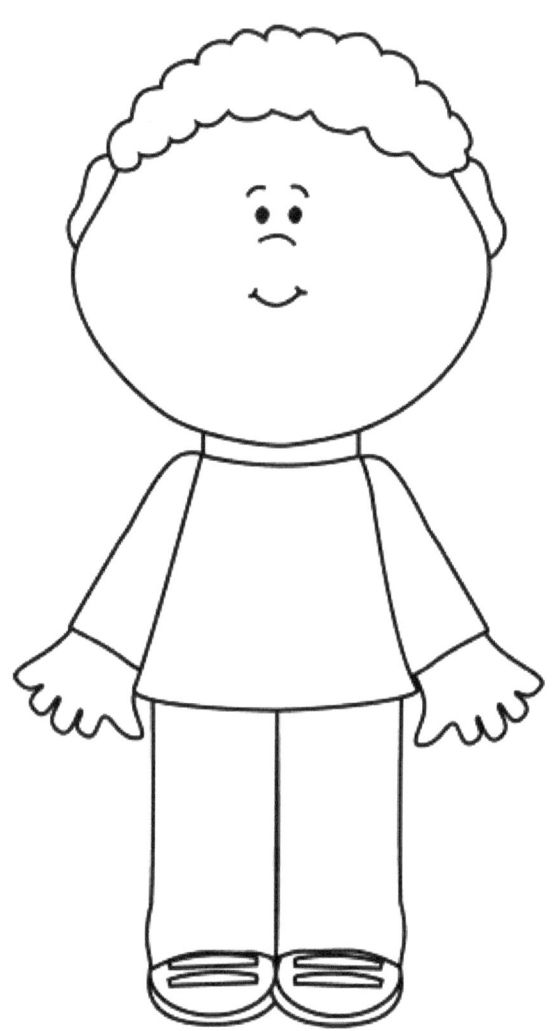

I LIKE SMILING.

(19)

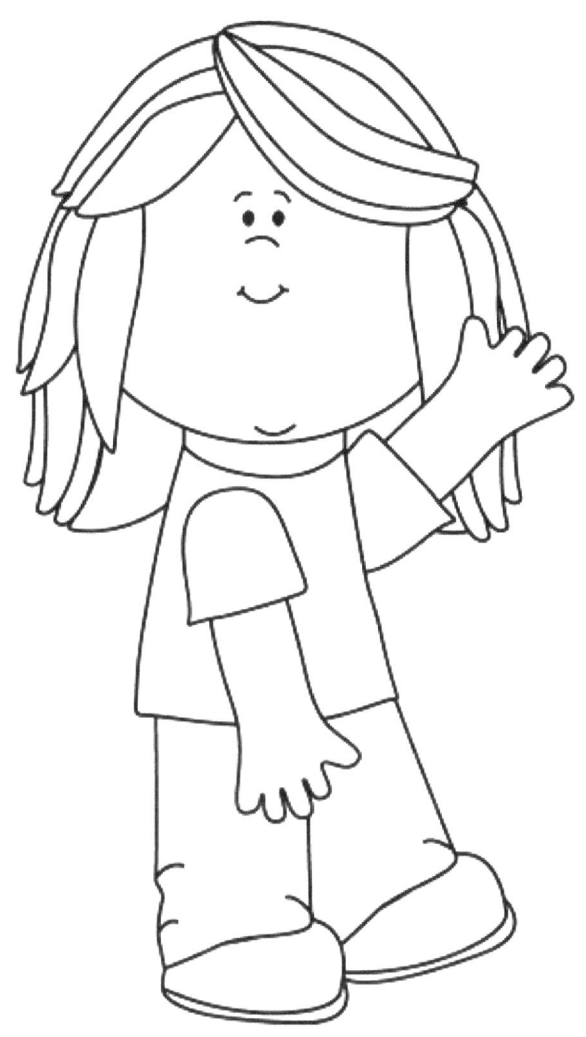

HELLO EVERYBODY!

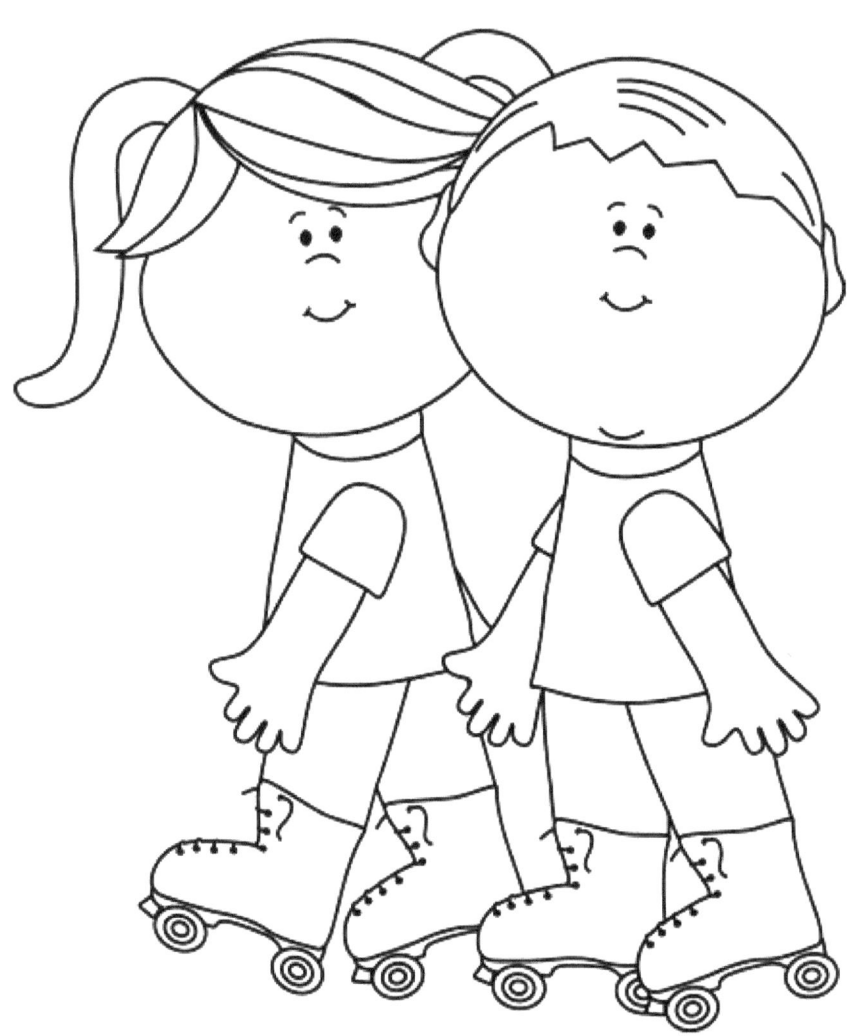

CAN YOU SKATE?

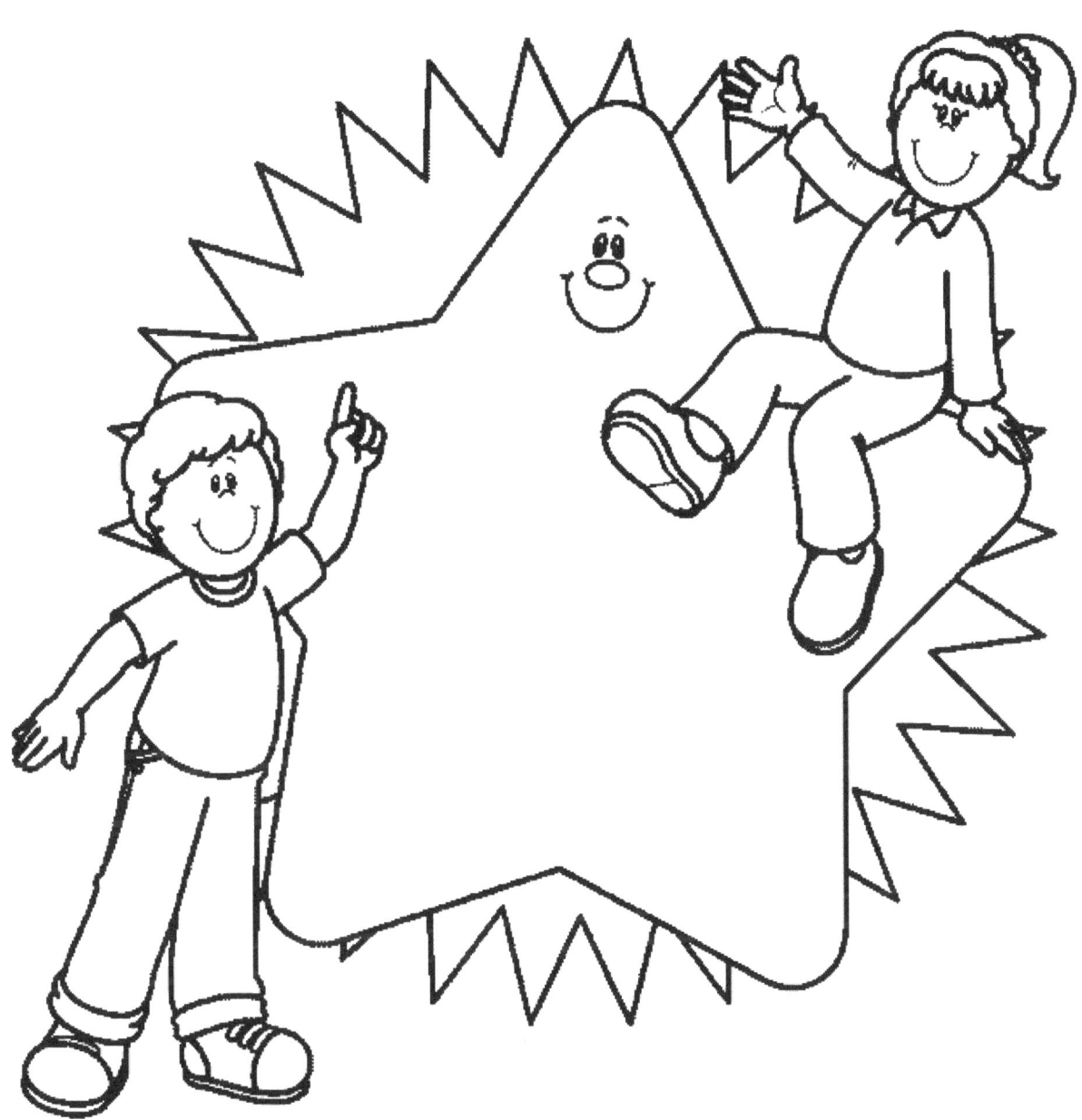

YOU'RE A STAR.

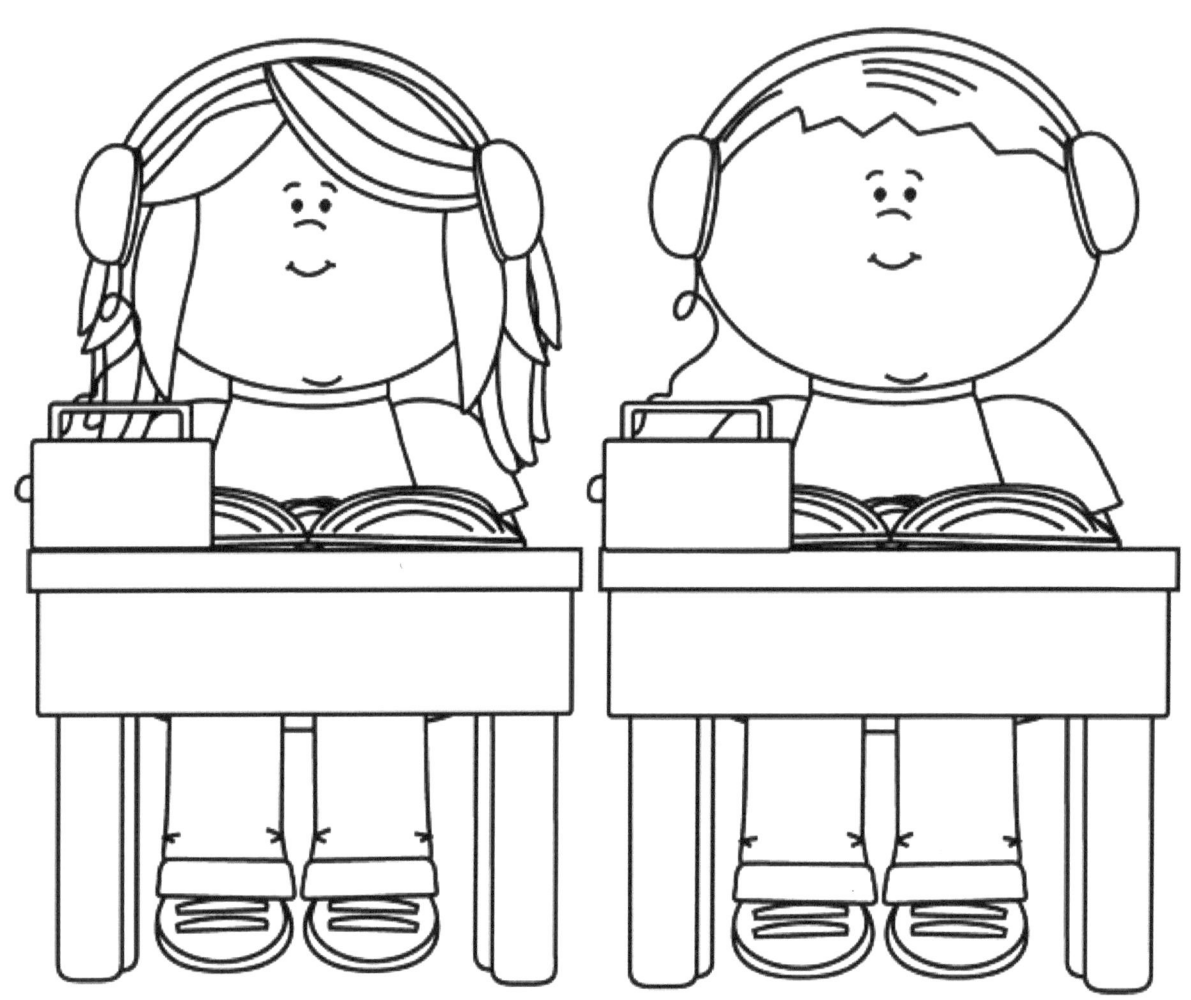

I LOVE GOING TO SCHOOL.

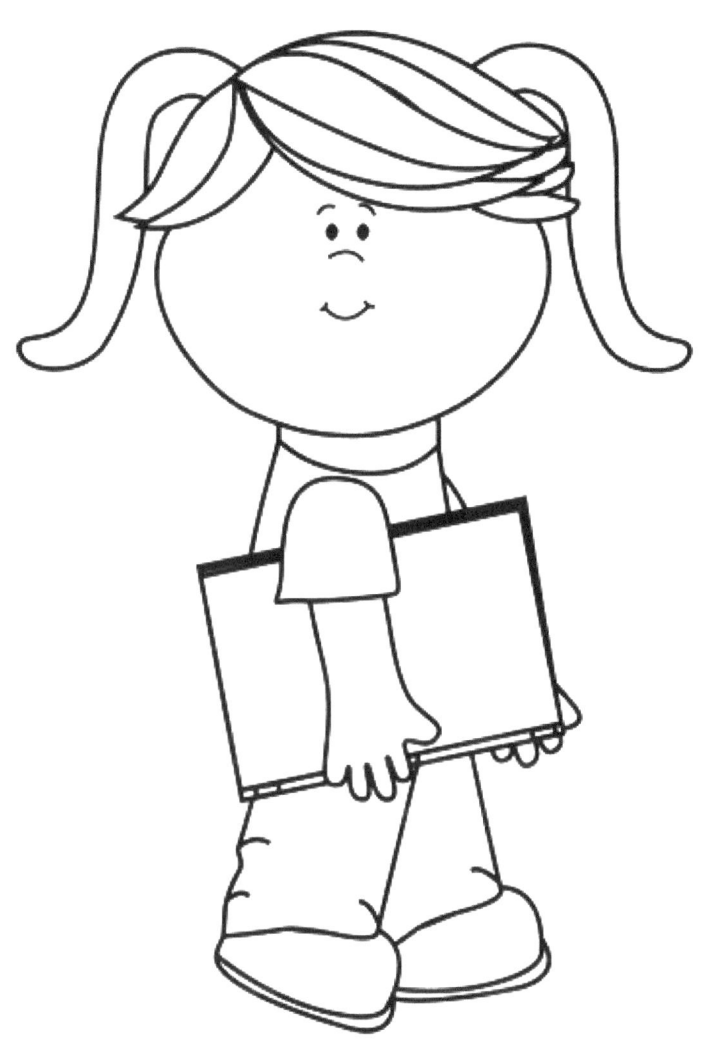

PLEASE GET YOUR EDUCATION BOYS AND GIRLS.